1994

STRESS
and the
SEARCH FOR
HAPPINESS

STRESS
and the
SEARCH FOR HAPPINESS

A New Challenge
for Christian Spirituality

Susan Muto and Adrian van Kaam

Resurrection Press
Mineola • New York

Imprimatur: Most Reverend Donald William Wuerl
Bishop of Pittsburgh
July 2, 1993

The Nihil obstat and the imprimatur are declarations that work is considered to be free from doctrinal or moral error. It is not implied that those who have granted the same agree with the contents, opinion or statements expressed.

Scripture selections are taken from the New American Bible.

First published in 1993 by Resurrection Press, Ltd.
P.O. Box 248
Williston Park, NY 11596

Copyright © 1993 by The Epiphany Association

ISBN 1-878718-17-7

Cover design and photograph by John Murello

Printed in the United States of America.

Contents

Introduction........................... 7

1. **Sources of Abnormal Stress** 9

2. **Normal Stress Enhances True Happiness** 17

3. **Scaling the Wall of Distress** 22

4. **Lessening Stress by Leaning on Christ** 27

5. **Seeing Stress as an Opportunity
   to Open Our Hearts to God** 30

6. **Distress Tempts Us to Cease
   Our Search for Happiness** 33

7. **Ordinary Stress in Relation to
   Our Divine Life Call** 36

8. **Obstacles That Retard Our Search** 39

9. **Conditions That Facilitate Our Search** 45

10. **Changing Distress into a Servant Source
     of Spiritual Formation** 51

Conclusion 56

Bibliography 59

Introduction

Everyone searches for happiness. Few seem to find it. Some have compared it to an elusive bird, and well they might. Millions of dollars are spent each year on vacations, cars, meals, entertainment, and consumer goods. Yet this abundance does not make people happy. To the contrary, it seems to leave many feeling stressed out and worn down. Why?

The answer is simple. These so-called satisfiers of desire promise us the world, but they do not deliver. It's as if we are trying to catch shadows. The harder we search for happiness, the more we get stuck in the quicksand of stress.

Are we facing an unresolvable dilemma? Must we give up the search for happiness to lessen stress? Must we conclude that stress is the price one pays for striving after a peaceful and productive life with God at its center? Is there a way to free ourselves, with the help of grace, from the horns of this dilemma?

That is the question we shall address in this book. It is the first in a Spirit Life Series of three texts in which we hope to tackle a topic crucial to Christian maturity, namely, the connection between stress and spirituality. Under the guidance of the Holy Spirit, we shall concentrate in this book on how stress can help rather than hamper our search for happiness. In the second publication, we shall show how to harness stress in concrete ways pertinent to the contemporary spiritual quest. In the third, we shall reflect on how to live a healthy and holy life under stress.

Before we begin, we would like to thank two special people who reduced our stress considerably by helping us in the concrete production of these texts, Marilyn Russell, our administrative assistant, and Karen Holttum, our expert typist.

1

Sources
of Abnormal Stress

Before we try to discover the link between normal stress and happiness, we have to uncover some of the sources of abnormal stress that invade modern life like a plague.

One does not have to be a physician or psychologist to realize that everyone regardless of age has some experience of stress. A teenager gets uptight if he does not have a date for the prom. A worker feels her stomach muscles contracting when her supervisor looks over her shoulder. A patient waits anxiously to receive the results of a diagnostic exam.

As a matter of fact the American Institute of Stress (AIS) reports that 75–90 percent of all visits to the doctor involve complaints that are stress-related. Thousands of people in America, to say nothing of the rest of the world, suffer from some form of abnormal stress.

If it is true that misery loves company, then we are not alone. Why has stress, which is almost as common as breathing, become an enemy rather than a partner in the search for happiness?

The amount of stress we feel at any one moment is not what diminishes or destroys our peace and joy. The problem of tense, anxious living stems not from stress as such but from our response to stressful situations. That, more than anything else, has an adverse affect on our happiness, health, and well being. We become, as it were, possessed or obsessed by our stress. This causes us nothing but trouble.

To become aware of why we feel so distraught, we need to pay more attention to the input that upsets us (for example, no date for the dance, supervision in the workplace, the outcome of an exam). These are typical sources of stress at certain times in the lives of certain people. At first glance they seem to be the opposite of happiness. What could they possibly have to do with our finding peace and joy or consonance with Christ?

Initial Responses to Stressful Situations

Lest you feel that you cannot dig your way out of the well into which stress has plunged you, here are a few wise moves you can make:

1. *Is it the situation or me?* Start by asking yourself, "What in this situation makes me feel so tense and unhappy? Am I taking things too seriously? Can I lighten up a bit? Is the situation causing me to feel this way or is my way of appraising what is going on making me feel so miserable?

   "What if the problem resides in me and not in something that is happening outside of me? Then I may begin to see in what direction the stress I am feeling is pointing.

   "Perhaps it is telling me, to return to our examples, 'I need to relax. If one friend says no to my request for a date, so what? There are other fish in the sea.' Or 'If I concentrate on doing my best, the boss will have no reason to reprimand me.' Or 'I cannot expect to be free of disease forever, given my family history. The outcome of the tests will remove any doubt I am having about my condition.' "

2. *What is my stress quotient?* The next thing to ask yourself is, "How much stress can I, in my uniqueness, with my responsibilities and limitations, reasonably bear?" Everyone is different in this regard. Mr. A, a creative artist, can tolerate more stress than Mr. B, a bartender with a short fuse.

"Know yourself" is one secret to overcoming abnormal stress. If you take upon your shoulders more stress than experience tells you that you can bear, then before long you can be sure stress will become distress. You will feel yourself slipping down the ski trail of overstress, heading for a collision.

3. *Do I have to do it all?* You need to ask yourself, "What makes me feel more stress than necessary?" Maybe you have a penchant to involve yourself in a veritable warehouse of extra activities: volunteer work, assignments over and above an already full schedule, family feuds you cannot resolve, trip after business trip with no rest in between.

All these extras may be justifiable in your mind, but it simply becomes too much. The more you do, the less contented you feel.

The solution for this kind of distress is simple, though it is difficult to implement. You have to stop it. You have to learn to say *NO* for the sake of a greater *YES* to true inner happiness. You have to know when you have reached your own "too much moment." Then you have to decide how you can best spend and expend your energy. What has to be done? What can be left undone?

The decision has less to do with the urgency of the

tasks facing you and more with your sense of how worthwhile it is to use up this kind of energy with no payback in peace of mind and lasting effectiveness.

4. *What triggers the tightness I feel?* You may be ready to face another key question: "Am I or am I not aware of what kinds of thoughts, feelings, or flights of fancy cause the normal stresses in modern life to overlap into distress for me?"

When the overlap happens, it is no fun. You have to track such triggers like a hunter stalks game. These trigger points disrupt your pace of life and reduce your peace. Once you discover that your actual inner response to stress is the cause of the pressure under which you are living, you have to find out how to dispel it.

5. *What is my body telling me?* Now ask, "Why do such feelings time and again have such a hold on my life? Do I have to be popular, pleasing, or preoccupied with what may go wrong, with evil, sickness, and death? Is there no other window through which to view life?"

You ought also to try to pinpoint how such moments of distress affect your chemical or vital-bodily reactions. Are you in a constant state of fight or flight?

Signals our body sends out are trustworthy indicators of distress, yet we often ignore or deny them until it is too late. Overstress wears us out. It can plunge us into low-grade depression. We feel headachy. Our back and shoulders are as tight as a violin string.

If this distress is allowed to continue, it will interfere with healthy, refreshing sleep. We may suffer before long from chronic fatigue. The more we rest, the more tired we feel. Other distress signals may be anxiety, night sweats, muscle pain, upset stomachs, or ulcers. Some of these symptoms require medical attention. They ought not to be denied.

We ought to take such physical symptoms seriously, especially when we have difficulty in admitting to ourselves that we are overstressed and unhappy. They are important indicators that our search for happiness may be taking us in the wrong direction. We have to turn our lives around.

Distress can be a warning signal that we have to return to normal stress before it is too late and we become hypertensive. Normal stress does not interfere with our search for true happiness. Becoming aware of our distress can be a first step toward naming the mental overload we have borne for longer than necessary.

6. *What feelings signal trouble?* If you have come this far in your self-diagnosis, you may want to become more

adept at identifying some of the feelings that signal distress. These might include: persistent doubts about the ultimate worthwhileness of life. This "what's the use" mentality may be rooted in weakening faith, diminished hope, and a tightening of the channels of giving and receiving love.

Neon signs signaling that overstress is afoot include insidious emotions of anger, hostility, irritability, resentment, envy, and unforgiveness as well as distrust and chronic suspicion. Watch out also if your sense of humor has become sarcastic or cynical.

This negative collection of emotions can add significantly to the degenerative shift from normal to abnormal distress. It goes without saying that such feelings cannot coexist with the search for happiness. At most, they point to deeper problems that have to do not with the quantity (so many prayers, so many devotions, so many worship services) but with the quality of our spiritual life.

As we shall see, in many cases the real cause of distress — why it retards the search for true happiness — is the lack of a serious yet relaxed and joyful presence to the mystery of Christ's love. He wants to take the burden of distress from our shoulders (cf. Mt 11:28–30).

The more we become aware of Christ as our friend

and redeemer, the more we will feel relief from useless worry. He will lift the weight of distress from us. We will see in short order what a world of difference that makes.

2

Normal Stress
Enhances True Happiness

So far we have seen how necessary it is to be on the alert for signs of distress. Moving on to the next stage of our journey, we can ask ourselves what it is like to feel consonance with Christ in the midst of the normal tugs and pulls of daily life?

It is our conviction that normal stress never interferes with the search for happiness. Indeed, stress can enhance this search on the condition that it helps us to be faithful to our unique-communal life call. In the process we learn to accept our limits and to live with the mistakes we make along the way. We avoid whatever seems to "Ease God Out," a popular way of saying that our "EGO" may incline us to forget that we are ultimately dependent on God to turn our distressed heart into a heart filled with true Christian peace and joy.

How do we know if we are on the way to replacing overstress by normal stress? Some sure signs of this shift might be these:

1. *Spontaneity.* Your thinking and acting become less forced and calculative, more spontaneous. You know when to laugh, when to cry, when to listen, when to speak. You are more in tune with what Christ would say and do in each situation. Everything about you is less tense and intense, less rigid, less removed from reality.

2. *Trust.* You are less prone to be judgmental about yourself and others due to unfounded fears and suspicions. You acknowledge that your former lack of trust was probably rooted in dread of failure, of being misunderstood by others, of being disliked by a stern God imagined in your fantasy as a judge who punishes anyone who does not perform perfectly. This heresy of perfectionism filled you with distress and blocked your search for happiness.

3. *Presence.* Instead of anxiously ruminating on the past, you feel able to let it go. You choose instead to enjoy to the full the events of your everyday life. You try to be present here and now to who you are and to what you are called to do. This gift of being present where you

are also diminishes your former inclinations to judge and condemn yourself and to deny your limits.

4. *Patience.* You notice yourself becoming more patient and kind. Your concerns for the words, actions, or possible thoughts and intentions of others ("Are they out to get me?") diminish dramatically. So, too, does your need to offer to yourself or others endless interpretations and analyses of what this or that event, person, or thing may mean. These mind-spinning activities used to exhaust you and cause nothing but abnormal stress. Now you are able to get off the merry-go-round of your mind and to rest in Christ's love. This by itself alone will lift a heavy load of distress from your shoulders and offer you new-found bliss and freedom.

5. *Detachment.* You will soon find yourself retreating from unnecessary conflict. You will know what is your cup of tea and what is your poison. You will be more detached, less preoccupied with unnecessary or imaginary distress caused by a conflicted mind and spirit. Not only outwardly but also inwardly, you will realize that some change is beginning to take place in you. No longer do you spin around in a useless circle of introspection or in a persistent debate about how or how not to resolve impossibly conflicted situations. You try the best you can to show

love and understanding, but you leave the outcome to God.

6. *Peace.* When your inner peace arises from the wellspring of Jesus' own gift of peace, you will be less inclined to worry (cf. Jn 14:27). It's as if feelings of depreciation that hung around you like smog over a seacoast town will start to dissipate. The winds of happiness blow away the storm clouds of useless distress.

7. *Appreciation.* Replacing these clouds of depreciation is the sunshine of warm appreciation. Distressing feelings that used to get the best of you, like dissonance and isolation, begin to give way to contented sighs of connectedness with God, with people and nature, with events and things. The smallest bush becomes as beautiful to you as the tallest tree. Your once frowning forehead and hang-dog face, a portrait of overstress, is now illumined by a smile that wells up straight from your heart.

8. *Freedom.* You realize that a great deal of what placed you under excessive stress may have been due to the fact that you felt the urge to control things or to make them happen only according to your own timetable or project. Now you are able to let things happen in their own good time and way. You have learned, as the saying goes, to let go and let God. Above all, you cease "Easing God

Out." No longer preoccupied with distress, your receptivity for love — now noticed by others — increases by leaps and bounds. "Whatever you are doing," a friend may say, "keep doing it. You're becoming really free and delightful."

Such signs of inner peace and joy, of energy and equanimity, can teach us a lesson in reverse. That is to say, their absence may mean we are at risk once again of falling into the snare of distress. Conflict and strife, if left unchecked, can leave us in the painful predicament of persistent stress. This is not what Jesus intended for us, to put it mildly. In fact, he said, "Do not be distressed or fearful" (Jn 14:27). And to those who believe, he gave this promise: "If you live according to my teaching, you are truly my disciples; then you will know the truth, and the truth will set you free" (Jn 8:31–32).

3

Scaling the Wall of Distress

$\mathbb{B}$y now it should be clear that the best way to grow beyond distress is to open up to the life of the spirit — that of us which goes beyond or transcends the limits of stressful functioning and draws us toward a redeeming path to happiness. The question is, why is it so hard for us to see disclosures of the Divine in our daily doings? Why aren't we more present to the revelation of God's love for us through his Son and our Savior, Jesus Christ?

Our stress-filled preoccupation with everything from paying bills to planning a vacation, from office demands to family celebrations, has built a barrier between us and the meanings and graces God wants to give us through the Holy Spirit. This wall has become so tall and thick that it seems to be an invincible obstacle to our search for happiness.

Once our life becomes walled off from God and any signs of his love, we become the prisoners of our own tensions and stresses. They are like stubborn jailers who taunt us with the promise of freedom only to cast us deeper into the pit.

Stress builds up to such a point that we feel isolated from self, others, and God. We become convinced that we have to climb over the wall under our own steam, but we do not know how. This build up of stress soon becomes abnormal. We are plunged into distress, frustrated in our search for happiness, and inclined to assume that it is normal to feel so uptight.

The truth is that we cannot break down the wall or instantly leap over it and enjoy the free space of transcendent living. This transformation takes time.

Seek Liberation in Christ

The first thing we can do to penetrate the wall of distress is to bore a few holes in it. Once it becomes porous, we can peek through it to the loveliness on the other side. We can catch a glimpse of the liberating way of Christ for which our hearts are aching.

Slowly and gradually we begin to experience the presence of the Holy Spirit in us as our Liberator. The Spirit wants to give us new strength and hope, together with a new appreciation for the here and now. We see everyday life less as an enemy and more as a friend inviting us to seek freedom of spirit in and with Christ.

Thus comes a decisive movement beyond the wall of distress behind which we have been hiding. It consists of our paying attention to those moments in which we are touched by the Holy Spirit. To attend to these invitations and challenges appreciatively, to flow with them, is to feel free again to pursue the life Jesus had in mind for us when he said: "No one who comes to me shall ever be hungry, no one who believes in me shall ever thirst" (Jn 6:35).

If we want to scale the wall of distress, we must remain present to Jesus in faith, hope, and love. In and through the Spirit, we will find the strength to persevere on the journey, even when we do not feel we are making much progress.

Something stirs in us — a new understanding, an inflow of energy — that awakens our slumbering or stressed heart. We have to be careful to treasure this awakening. We must not dismiss it as frivolous. This stirring is a grace of God. It assuages our distress to recall Jesus's words, "I will not leave you orphaned" (Jn 14:18). If only for a short while, we can breathe a sigh of relief.

It is as if a knapsack full of stones has been lifted from our shoulders. We sense that we do not have to do it alone. Our search for Christian happiness is sustained by the Holy Spirit. We are being led to a Christ-likeness that will help us to overcome many obstacles, including our scaling the wall of distress that nearly destroyed our hope of happiness.

Christ's plenitude and power create in us a new sense of possibility. The wall almost seems to be made of rubber rather than of rock. What used to separate us from life's transcendent meaning now seems to be a bridge to the land of freedom and likeness to the Lord. We see other ways to scale the wall. In fact, life, which had taken an overly serious turn lacking any sense of play, is now seen as a playground in which we and God are partners and co-creators.

Choose to Hope

Another way to scale the wall is to see suffering and disappointment not only as causes of distress but as occasions for seeking deeper meaning. We reject the option of despair and choose hope. Once again we shun the cloud of depreciation and turn our faces to the sun of appreciation.

This inner turning toward the transcendent becomes more and more habitual to us. Though we feel the normal stress anyone would under such circumstances, we do not cave in to distress. We begin to scale the wall whereas before we would cringe before its massiveness or shudder in its shadow.

We may find it hard to grasp with our limited minds what is

happening to us. Why this change? Why this subtle lessening of fear? Why this restoration of possibility?

Aided by grace, we begin to accept that the Spirit can help us to make sense out of what others see only as nonsense. We come to believe that in every obstacle there resides a formation opportunity.

This conviction diminishes abnormal stress dramatically. It is an essential step in the search for lasting happiness. Our small, stressed-out minds, exhausted by figuring and planning, come to rest. Uplifted by faith and illumined by the mind of Christ, we are drawn to a higher level of seeing and believing (cf. Jn 20:29).

4

Lessening Stress
by Leaning on Christ

With this first general phase of liberation behind us, we are ready to move to a new level in the removal of distress for the sake of realizing our God-given call to happiness in Christ. We cannot emphasize enough the importance of remaining present to the cross and the resurrection in times of suffering and disappointment.

This Christ-presence begins to resound in us not only in times of contemplation but at every turn in the road of ordinary life. We no longer settle for a mere pragmatic or functional way of understanding. We want to know precisely what opposes our best attempts to worship God in spirit and truth (cf. Jn 4:24).

There dawns in us a new-found faith in the hidden power of God's reign in our life and world. We may have told the Lord perfunctorily of our love, but only through this struggle with stress have we come to understand the truth that "Love has no room for fear; rather, perfect love casts out all fear (1 Jn 4:18).

Strengthened by grace, we begin to appreciate the degree to which we are being embraced and led by the Holy Spirit to the place prepared for us by God (cf. Jn 14:1–4). Of what significance is the downswing of distress compared to the upswing of grace? It makes us receptive and open to the Risen Lord. Jesus wants us to lean on him. We don't have to make it in this world alone. We can trust in Christ to catapult us over the walls of anxious concern that used to bind our freedom.

The world with its stress-filled strivings for position, power, pleasure, and possession as ultimate sources of joy may mock our faith and call us naive. The Holy Spirit assures us that we can be in this world without being of it (cf. Jn 17:14–16). We can meet every obligation with fervent dedication, but without distress, because we believe we are being overshadowed by the wings of God's protective love (cf. Ps 36:8).

Such liberating experiences signal the turning point in a stressful life. They are the keys by which to unlock the inmost Christ-form of our soul. As we center ourselves in the Lord, we will calm down. Tension unwinds. We relativize the importance of our cleverness and efficiency. It has only gotten us in trouble. We see that modes of mastery have come to naught compared to the effectiveness that is ours when we listen to the mystery, to the still small voice of the Spirit within us.

This experience of the lessening of stress may happen with special intensity when the script we have written for our life simply does not play. A child almost dies in a car accident. A wife dearly loved announces she wants a divorce. A job we counted on goes to someone else. A vacation we planned turns out to be a disaster.

Stress rises to a fever pitch at such times. We wanted nothing more than to live in comfort and security. Now look at what has happened. Old walls crumble and new ones arise. Is it any wonder we see no way across the wall but to lean on Jesus. For, as he says, "I am the gate. Whoever enters through me will be safe" (Jn 10:9).

5

Seeing Stress
as an Opportunity
to Open Our Hearts to God

If we are serious about searching for true happiness, we cannot conclude that collapse is the end of the line. We cannot refuse to renew the process of dismantling the wall, if only brick by brick. Our survival as a person is at stake. We have to believe as never before in the life of the Risen Lord in us.

In these times of deepest need, the God who loves us first may appear to us in a whole new way (cf. 1 Jn 4:10). Divine grace begins to mitigate our distress the moment we turn to God for help. Through the power of faith, we may be able to accept as a formation opportunity what once only seemed to be an obstacle.

We may see the way over the wall Christ challenges us to take, for he said, "I am the way, and the truth, and the life" (Jn

14:5). We may sense, much to our astonishment, that Christ is lifting us beyond the stones of distress as a pulley raises a weighty bucket from a well.

This comforting awareness of Christ's life in us makes it possible for us to cope with one of the underlying causes of abnormal stress or distress. Everyone of us will die, no matter how we may try to deny this inescapable fact of life. Who of us has not felt distressed at the thought of death? Our life here and now seems so meaningless, so small, when it is placed against the "big picture." This can drive us to cringe behind the wall, hugging ourselves into a ball of sadness, if not despair.

To say the least, it is difficult to search for happiness when the thought of life as meaningless or as merely a useless suffering overtakes us. At times nothing helps but to take a giant leap of faith over the wall.

When the dark cloud of depreciation rolls over the desert of our heart, our normal range of stress looks like the Sahara. Why should we bear with everyday stress if all we do ends in the distress of death? If this feeling of our being abandoned by God takes precedence in our life, we may find no way over the wall of distress. Suicide may seem like the only viable alternative.

Now it is imperative to connect with the greater life of Christ in us. The peaks and valleys of our existence are passing. The Cross of Christ is lasting. We are little words in the

Divine Word. Our existence may be finite, but we can be sure that with the Risen Christ we will live forever. As Jesus told Martha to relieve the distress she felt because her brother Lazarus was dead: "I am the resurrection and the life: whoever believes in me, though he should die, will come to life; and whoever is alive and believes in me will never die" (Jn 11:25–26).

The sting of death dissipates in the light of the divinity and humanity of Christ in whose image or form we have been made, in whose name we have been baptized.

This experience of God's nearness to us melts down the massive mountain of overstress our minds may build up when we are out of touch with the mystery. This is not to say that faith works like magic. Tragic loss remains tragic loss, but from the beginning God has readied the graces we need to cope with distress in such a way that it does not block our God-given search for happiness.

In this way we see stress as an opportunity to open our hearts to the God who loves and sustains us in sickness and in health. With Job we can say, "The Lord gave and the Lord has taken away; blessed be the name of the Lord!" (Jb 1:21).

6

Distress Tempts Us to Cease Our Search for Happiness

Once we learn to welcome everyday stresses as opportunities given to us by God to participate in the reign of Christ in this world, we have to be on the alert.

Distress will tempt us to stop our search. The demonic does not want us to take part in the dying and rising of Christ for the sake of our salvation and that of all people of good will.

At such moments of temptation, we are out of tune with the sacred. The tyranny of our profane way of coping with suffering tends to take precedence over God's purpose. Our need to justify and understand every iota of the mystery — as did Job — closes our ears to the voice of God in the whirlwind of distress (cf. Jb 38:1–7). These hours of being tested by grace can be our finest. As we learn to listen with new ears and respond to

33

God with a new heart, we may taste something of the joyful
confidence in God of which the psalmist speaks:

> *When I call, answer me, O my just God,*
>   *you who relieve me when I am in distress;*
>   *Have pity on me, and hear my prayer!*
>
> .   .   .   .
>
>   *for you alone, O Lord,*
>   *bring security to my dwelling.*
>
> Ps 4:2, 9

For this reason it should not surprise us to discover that the
demonic, the prince of darkness and deception, wants nothing
more of us than that we remain behind the wall of distress and
unhappiness, wallowing in self-pity, anger, and depression.

This climate of distress makes it easier for the devil to tempt
us to give up hope in Christ and to rely on our own cleverness.
When our faith is weakened due to tension and sadness, we
are vulnerable to the demonic who wants to prevent at any
price the transforming of our distress by Christ. Therefore, the
powers of darkness make us question the truth of the promise
of liberation in and through our Lord.

Now more than ever we must not give up hope. We must
pray that the Holy Spirit will raise us beyond any demonic
temptation to stop the search. Being on the way does not mean
that we will escape the normal pain and suffering that belong

to any human life. Nothing is perfect. However, it is possible to experience moments of transcendent joy the demonic cannot attack and destroy. Such moments go beyond the passing pleasures of bodily gratification or the attained ambitions of functional satisfaction and have about them the flavor of the Infinite.

It is consoling to know that gifts of high illumination are not necessary for redeeming everyday distress. More important are the times when the Holy Spirit may touch us almost imperceptibly. The more open we are to such simple touches of the Divine, the more receptive we will be to their recurrence. It is as if our radar for the mystery in the midst of everydayness has been charged with a new battery.

Such ordinary encounters can be epiphanic. They weaken the hold the demonic may have on our distressed heart. They make our everyday stresses seem meaningful and more tolerable.

7

Ordinary Stress in Relation to Our Divine Life Call

The touches of which we have been speaking are neither the results of intense meditation nor of ecstatic or extraordinary illumination. Were they of such a lofty nature, they might interfere with the task at hand and add to our burdens yet another source of stress!

Rather these touches of the Transcendent come to us quietly and leave us as quietly. They do not interrupt our work in the least. We feel peace in the midst of productivity.

The grace of God enables us to see in a new light the ordinary demands and stresses associated with our daily tasks. We become more agile in our actions. We are less likely to have our feathers ruffled by every setback. We seem to be able to draw upon an inner abundance of grace. We keep our two feet on the ground but do not trip over the gravel. We have a lighter step and a lighter heart. We feel more whole and content with what we are doing here and now. At the same time we sense the meaning of our role in the ongoing process of transformation of cosmos and humanity by the Risen Lord.

We have come to see that the search for happiness is less about finding something or someone outside of us and more about trusting Christ within us and in others. Through these small workaday events of divine nearness, we become aware of the deeper meaning of our life. We learn to let go of the holding power of everyday stresses and to take them in stride. We see Christ in a new light. He is our liberator, the friend who has freed us from the fetters of our functional consciousness while rooting us in the firm soil of our divine life call.

This call has be heard in and through the tensions of everyday living if it is to remain as real as the Nazareths and Jerusalems of Jesus' own life. In due time we may see, wherever we look, compelling evidence of the cosmic Christ whose life in us far surpasses our limited sojourn on earth.

Since baptism we belong in essence to the eternal omnipresence of Christ in us and others. We live at once in two orders of reality: the temporal and the eternal. This is a truth known and lived by such spiritual giants as Augustine, Benedict, Catherine of Siena, John of the Cross, Teresa of Avila, Francis Libermann, Søren Kierkegaard, Evelyn Underhill, and T. S. Eliot, to mention only a few.

In our baptized being we are made one with Christ. This revelation is the goal of our formation, the end point of our search for happiness, the resolution of negative stress. How, then, can we live in its light? Are there some basic obstacles to and conditions for scaling the wall of distress once and for all?

8

Obstacles That Retard Our Search

In the light of our aim to search for happiness in the midst of stress, two obstacles loom large. They are *willfulness* and *will-lessness*. Both block our search. Both lead to excessive stress.

Willfulness means living in a condition that is full of tense stubborn control by our lower will. It is not enlightened by transcendent life directives emanating from the union between our higher spiritual will and the Divine Will. Instead our lower will, in anxious control, separates us from the Christ life in the depth of our being. Out of touch with our spiritual will, we are likely to succumb to the pressures associated with merely managing willfulness.

Our concerns to execute our own will in set plans and projects, our fear of anyone or anything that may threaten what we want, put us under exhausting stress. We pray to the Lord, "Thy will be done," but we think secretly, "according to my script." We are bound by willfulness to hide behind a grid of defenses. We feel compelled to fulfill our security needs, no matter what. It is as if we see a threat on every corner. We cannot bear to feel that we might be losing control.

Willfulness causes us to be on edge. We do not dare to relax. This network of fears and defenses is a breeding ground for distress. Such extra stress goes far beyond the demands of daily life. It leads to distress in short order.

The obstacle of will-lessness can be as harmful to our search for happiness as its opposite, willfullness. Will-less persons are as slack as willful persons are tense. They lack the will to disclose their life call and to implement its directives. Will-less persons prefer to let the "roll of the dice" take over their lives. They do not want to make decisions or to commit themselves to a course of action that is in tune with God's unique will in the here and now situation. They pray to the Lord, "Thy will be done" with no realistic sense of the situation, without so much as an outline of a script inspired and supported by the Spirit.

Will-less types lack the decisiveness and courage necessary for dealing with the stresses everyone who wants to live an effective and productive life must meet. This kind of flabbiness is in itself a source of added stress.

One may think that laid-back people are free from stress in any form. One may look at them with envy, but look again. Missing the courage and stamina to cope with the ups and downs of everyday life makes even normal stress an opening to distress. It appears more formidable than it is. It can bowl one over. Every setback is magnified beyond proportion. Ordinary stresses become overwhelming distresses.

Dissonant Effects of These Obstacles

Victims of these two obstacles to the search for happiness may experience a constant swing from willfulness to will-lessness. This see-saw effect is itself exhausting. The swing from being overly controlling to not wanting to be in charge of anything prevents the stable formation of the central core, heart or character of a person called to image the heart of Christ.

Lack of character makes it hard for us to cope with the stresses and tensions that challenge us from the time we get out of bed in the morning to when we retire at night.

Once we accept that we have to change or else risk losing our health and happiness, we may have no choice but to turn to Christ for help. He will show us the way. He will give us the strength to overcome these two grave obstacles to our character formation.

What we need to cultivate in imitation of Christ is a stable heart that is neither overstressed nor understressed. The balance is not easy to come by. It takes time and patience for all of us.

In the grip of willfulness we may find that excessive self-will ("I want what I want when I want it"); relentless self-control ("I should always be in charge everywhere"); and continual surveillance by an all-too-watchful managing-*I* ("Nothing escapes my tense attention") takes its toll.

In the grip of will-lessness we may be overcome by apathy ("It makes no difference what I do"); paralyzing complacency ("I don't want to make waves"); and an unwillingness to take initiative ("I'm too bored to do anything but wait for tomorrow").

Both of these obstacles block the flow of the inspirations of the Holy Spirit and our corresponding aspirations. An inexorable tension builds in mind and body when such stirrings of grace are pushed to the background and our willful plans and projects or our will-less inertia rule the roost.

Cultivating Consonant Dispositions

Distrustful willfulness and its inclination to excessive self-reliance have to give way to our becoming more trustful persons. Are we confident of the life-giving and liberating

Christ-form within us since baptism? Are we willing to become in Christ a new creation (cf. Eph 4:24).

It is safe to say that all distress that results from willfulness shows a lack of trust in Christ's power to free us from sin and to give us a new start.

Will-lessness, by contrast, is a sign that we have given up the search for spiritual happiness in fidelity to the call of Christ. It is as if we refuse to accept the responsibility we bear to make our lives meaningful, effective, and productive. Are we ready to pursue Christian excellence? Are we willing to remain true to our call to use the gifts God has given us? Are we able to meet the challenges of daily life?

If there is an answer to this tug of war between willfulness and will-lessness, it may lie in our willingness to shape a core form or character that is receptive to as well as responsible for dealing with the stresses from which normal living is never freed.

The disposition of trustful abandonment ("I don't have to do it alone") goes hand in hand with the disposition of creative dedication ("God helps those who help themselves"). Without these dispositions, the search for true happiness may degenerate into a stressful reaction to happenstance.

In due course doubt begins to weaken our conviction of Christ's care. We pray less and complain more. We are not transparent expressions to others of the unique Christ-form meant for our lives and theirs. Neither do we strive to fulfill the mission, task, or service God meant for us from all eternity.

If we continue to follow the wrong road, we take the risk that happiness will elude us. To prevent this from happening, we need to focus on conditions that facilitate our search without adding to the normal stress we can bear. Whatever we do, we ought to follow the counsel of the Apostle Paul: "Be imitators of God as his dear children. Follow the way of love, even as Christ loved you" (Eph 5:1–2).

9

Conditions That Facilitate Our Search

To cultivate conditions that facilitate our search for happiness in the midst of stress may seem as simple as planting bulbs guaranteed to bloom in the spring. The trouble is that we humans, unlike plants, have a free will that can resist the soundest sayings of common sense.

The Lord told us not to be anxious about tomorrow since each day has its own concerns. Why worry? It does not add one inch to our life. "If the smallest things are beyond [our] power, why be anxious about the rest" (Lk 12:26)?

It might seem easy to acquire this sensitivity to the reality God allows in our life. In fact it takes long practice to be at home with the undiluted *"givenness"* of our here and now experience. It takes patience to enjoy the day-after-dayness of life's unfolding and to "stop worrying" (Lk 12:29).

Why is common sense such a rarity? Why do many opt instead to become "holy floaters" or "pious plodders," swinging from idle illusions to rigid rules?

The truth is that our minds and hearts are overflowing with thoughts and concerns for family life and work, for the future, for our financial stability, for every scenario under the sun. We are intimidated by input from the media, by a flood of self-help books and attitudes, by a proliferation of talk shows and entertainment sources.

We also have to cope with the inner clutter of prejudices carried over from childhood conversations at the kitchen table, on the porch, and in front of the T.V. Our interiority is like a mile-high filing cabinet full of ideas and theories of the what-ifs and what-if-nots of endless speculation.

All of this clutters up our minds like furniture stuffed into an already overcrowded room. Covered with dust are the conditions of spontaneity, trust, and presence that dispose us to fight the good fight, finish the race, and keep the faith (cf. 2 Ti 4:7).

Such conditions make us attentive to the need to put Christ first. He said, "Do not live in fear, little flock" (Lk 12:32). Such sacred words are stress reducers. They relieve the denseness of distressed minds and put us in touch with the never failing love of God. They free us from the tyranny of tense oughts and narrow shoulds.

Matter-of-factness and sobriety, everyday "horse sense" or common wisdom are conditions for inner rest. They enable us to accept that the God who clothes in splendor the grass of the field, which grows today and tomorrow is thrown on the fire, will provide for us (cf. Lk 12:28). This truth encourages us to make the best of a sometimes bad deal and not to make a mountain out of a molehill.

Stress-Reducing Intimacy with God

The search for Christian happiness disposes us, therefore, to stay with what is, as it is, and to see the given as a gift of God. We are as ready to thank God for the blessing of joy as we are to accept the burden and challenge of suffering.

Without this attunement to reality, our spiritual life risks becoming a matter of routinized churchgoing rather than a person-to-person relationship with God and with other pilgrims on the way.

In the end, the most foundational condition that facilitates our search for happiness is to live in warm, loving intimacy with the mystery that sustains and embraces us and others. Without love we cannot hope to overcome the obstacles that arise from abnormal stress, including our vulnerability to the powers of darkness.

Love shields us from the shadows of tension, lack of trust and anxious rumination. Love compels us to listen with inner ears to the consoling words of the beloved disciple, John, who says:

Little children,
let us love in deed and in truth
and not merely talk about it.
This is our way of knowing we are committed to the truth
and are at peace before him
no matter what our consciences may charge us with;
for God is greater than our hearts
and all is known to him.

1 Jn 3:18–20

Faith-Filled Presence to Distress

Faith shows us the way to escape the prison of unhappiness and tension that unfortunately seems to be more the rule than the exception in modern life. Faith enables us to follow the way of Jesus Christ. It nourishes our capacity for intimacy with God and others. It helps us to "nip in the bud" any sign of excessive stress and lift it into the light of the Transcendent.

This way of "going beyond" or "lifting up" does not tempt

us to escape from reality. Neither does it demand a proliferation of mental or physical exercises to reduce stress as such. While such techniques may put Band-Aids on the wounds of a stressed life, they are not preventive medicine, nor do they, by themselves alone, liberate us from a stressed-out life style.

Only one exercise can do that. It is to repeat to ourselves the basic truth that through each here and now event in daily life God offers us the best opportunity to assess the meaning of distress. We are to rise above it by opting to take stress in stride and never to let it subdue our consonance with Christ.

In this way, all people, events, and things, however distressful they may be, can be seen as openings to practice the ancient yet ever animating art of living in faith-filled presence to the here and now as a gift of God.

This practice of the presence of God, to use the phrase coined by Brother Lawrence of the Resurrection, should become second nature to us. After some time we ought to find ourselves spontaneously distinguishing between normal and abnormal stress like a barometer picks up alterations in air pressure. If it helps, we can even talk to ourselves saying, "There I go again, buying a ticket to the merry-go-round of distress when it doesn't add a cubit to the fulfillment of my life call."

Frequently during the day we ought also to ask ourselves, "Am I being faithful to the Christ life in me since baptism?"

This becomes our checkpoint. Even if we fail, we live in the faith-inspired conviction of Christ's forgiveness and unfailing support.

This practice transforms our overstressed life step by step. It gives us a peace the world cannot give, a peace that, as the Apostle Paul says, surpasses understanding (cf. Phil 4:7). It leads us to a place and posture of joyous presence to the Lord. We become living expressions of Christ's care and concern.

No longer obsessed or possessed by distress, we catch a glimpse of the horizon of our search for happiness. We enter into the land of likeness to the Divine from whence we have drifted and to which in faith we hope to return.

10

Changing Distress into a Servant Source of Spiritual Formation

Besides learning to accept everyday reality as God's gift, which is a great stress reducer, we need to move toward the ultimate goal of faith: to change distress into a servant source of formation. Helping us to do so are three concrete practices all of us can follow:

1. *Reiteration.* Rather than becoming discouraged when distress periodically overwhelms us, rather than blaming someone else for our problems, we can repeat to ourselves the faith-filled conviction that every mistake we make has a meaning. It may tell us that we are slipping back to our old ways of willfulness or will-lessness. This happens when a person is under pressure. Deformed dis-

positions die hard! That is why we have to say again and again that no problem life presents ought to distress us to the point of depression and certainly not to the point of despair. There is always room for redemption from distress, no matter what happens.

If we repeat this simple truth, then our daily round of work *in* the world can be at the same time an occasion for working *on* ourselves. With the help of grace, we can begin reforming flawed dispositions that drive us into distress.

The most important part of this inner work is to discover why we are so tense and upset. What is causing us to feel this way? Have we fallen back into patterns of fight or flight? Is useless worry wearing us out? What is blocking our formation energy? How can we restart its flow?

Without the gift of reiteration, we would neither ask the right questions nor seek the best stress-reducing responses. Reiteration, like a prayer refrain, makes it possible for us to identify the sources of excessive stress and to cope wisely with them. Repeatedly attuning ourselves to life as a formation opportunity teaches us that we, not others, are the main cause of the stress that distresses us. Slowly and gradually we begin to see that ordinary ups and downs can be changed from obstacles that stand in the way of our attunement to grace into opportunities for lasting growth.

2. *Resolve.* A second condition for preventing distress from getting the best of us is resolve. This means that we make a firm commitment to do what has to be done to meet our obligations and to secure our relations in a way that does not betray our unique-communal life call.

Such resolve requires steady vigilance. If we deny or betray our call, we feel unhappy. Something is out of order. Inordinate stress creeps up on us like a stranger in the night. The more it accumulates, the more we must resolve to return to a posture of fidelity. Of what use is it to waste energy fighting or fleeing from who we are called to be? It is hard enough to cope with the normal stresses lodged in daily life without wasting precious energy trying to suppress our call.

Resolving to remain faithful to the Lord who calls us by name (cf. Is 41:25; 62:2; and 63:19) liberates us from the misuse of formation energy. We are able to manage stress without fearing that it will master us.

3. *Resistance.* Healthy stress helps us to resist values, directives, and traditions that are alien to our commitment to uphold and live by the counsels and beatitudes of the Gospel.

The world in its worldliness teaches us from early childhood that gain is everything. This inclination to consume and to possess contaminates, as perhaps nothing else can, our practice of stress liberation and our search for Christian happiness.

We may even apply the same mentality of gain to prayer experiences, as if the more ecstasy we have, the more peace we can commandeer. Projects of self-salvation or perfectionism prompt a similar course.

This kind of pressure generates only new stress, not happiness. Spirituality becomes yet another thing we do. Before long, it becomes a stress indicator rather than a stress liberator. We fall victim to the principle of double effect. We become stressed about being distressed. We target stress as an imperfection we hate and despise, as an enemy to destroy rather than as a force to befriend.

Spirituality of this sort will have no effect whatsoever on the reduction of unnecessary stress. It is simply one more item of business we have to add to an already overburdened life.

Another worldly value, alien to the way of Jesus, which we ought to resist, is the satisfying of surface wants and needs at the expense of remaining present to the deeper mysteries of life and death.

We need to open our minds to these eternal truths. We have to bring our hearts into contact with the living God. Otherwise life will remain a routine, boring affair, an endless round of buying and selling, having and doing. Religion may be at most a pious collection of dos and don'ts without an inner treasure of prayer and presence.

The world in its worldliness will always push us toward activism and measurable results, mostly monetary. We buy into the pressure to keep busy, even at the risk of forfeiting the happiness for which our hearts long. We fall victim to the expectation that we have to pursue any person or thing that promises to diminish distress.

Gain new knowledge and skills. Buy more goods. Build bigger houses. Purchase more expensive cars. This litany of false promises cannot deliver lasting gifts of peace and joy. It has to be resisted. The danger of indiscriminate consumerism is that it becomes mixed up with the search for happiness whereas for most people it is only an ever-present source of counterproductive stress.

Conclusion

To allow God's loving will into this worldliness and to act in accordance with it requires a true leap of faith. It feels as if we must scale a wall as high as a Wall Street skyscraper. Happiness lies on the other side but a world that worships activism and consumerism does not want us to see that. Rather we are told that happiness is to be found on the merry-go-round of an unreflective, immature existence.

No wonder we feel overstressed! What else should we expect? This condition is the result of our buying blindly into illusory promises of happiness and shutting down our search for the real thing.

The real thing begins when we remember the words of the Lord: "Come to me, all you who are weary and find life burdensome, and I will refresh you. Take my yoke upon your shoulders and learn from me, for I am gentle and humble of heart. Your souls will find rest, for my yoke is easy and my burden light" (Mt 11:28–30).

In these words Jesus invites us to turn within, to listen to life with the ears of our heart. Unburdened by overstress, we can engage in social service or any other enterprise without feeling we have to do it all. Jesus calls us to do our best, not to worry and fret about what has be left undone.

Jesus wants us to lead a blessed life in the midst of stress without breaking down or becoming addicted, without building our house on the loose sands of passing possessions we cannot own permanently (cf. Mt 7:26–27).

With this goal in mind, let us pray:

Good Shepherd, though at times we may feel lost and forlorn, help us to find our way home to the pasture of your presence where happiness reigns supreme.

Crucified, glorified Lord, when stress threatens to become distress, wrap us tightly in your outstretched arms and help us to grow calm.

God of Abraham, Isaac, and Jacob, let us become signs of your covenant of love with a recalcitrant people, always in need of forgiveness.

King of kings, make us worthy to celebrate the paschal feast in the company of your disciples.

Trinity Divine, teach us the way of wonder and gratitude.

Spirit of Love, let us never forget that you are forever calling us home to a new and more abundant life.

Amen.

Bibliography

Augustine, St. *The Confessions of St. Augustine*. Trans. John K. Ryan. Garden City, NY: Doubleday and Co., 1960.

Blythe, Peter. *Stress: The Modern Sickness*. London: Pan Books Ltd., 1975.

Catherine of Siena, St. *The Dialogue*. Trans. Suzanne Noffke, O.P. *Classics of Western Spirituality Series*. New York: Paulist Press, 1980.

Eliot, T. S. *The Complete Poems and Plays, 1909–1950*. New York: Harcourt, Brace & World, 1934.

Gilbert, Alphonse. *You Have Laid Your Hand On Me....* Rome: Spiritan Research and Animation Centre, 1983.

John of the Cross, St. *The Collected Works*. Trans. Kieran Kavanaugh, O.C.D., and Otilio Rodriguez, O.C.D. Washington, DC: Institute of Carmelite Studies, 1973.

Kierkegaard, Søren. *Purity of Heart Is to Will One Thing*. Trans. D. Steere. New York: Harper & Row, 1956.

Lawrence of the Resurrection, Brother. *The Practice of the Presence of God*. Trans. Donald Attwater. Springfield, IL: Templegate, 1976.

Muto, Susan. *Blessings That Make Us Be*. New York: Crossroad, 1982.

_____. *Meditation in Motion*. New York: Image Books, 1986.

Owens, Virginia Stem. *And The Trees Clap Their Hands: Faith, Perception, and the New Physics.* Grand Rapids, MI: William B. Eerdmans Publishing Company, 1983.

The Rule of St. Benedict. Trans. Abbot Justin McCann. London: Sheed and Ward, 1972.

Seligman, Martin E. P. *Learned Optimism.* New York: Pocket Books, Div. of Simon and Schuster, 1990.

Selye, Hans. *The Stress of Life.* New York: McGraw-Hill Book Company, 1956.

Teresa of Avila, St. *The Collected Works.* Trans. Kieran Kavanaugh, O.C.D., and Otilio Rodriguez, O.C.D. Washington, DC: Institute of Carmelite Studies, 1976.

Underhill, Evelyn. *Practical Mysticism.* Columbus, OH: Ariel Press, 1942.

van Kaam, Adrian. *Spirituality and the Gentle Life.* Denville, NJ: Dimension Books, 1974.

———. *A Light to the Gentiles: The Life Story of the Venerable Francis Libermann.* Denville, NJ: Dimension Books, 1959.

———. *Spirituality and the Gentle Life.* Denville, NJ: Dimension Books, 1974.

———. *Looking for Jesus.* Denville, NJ: Dimension Books, 1978.

———. *The Mystery of Transforming Love.* Denville, NJ: Dimension Books, 1982.

———. *Roots of Christian Joy.* Denville, NJ: Dimension Books, 1985.

———. *The Transcendent Self: Formative Spirituality of the Middle, Early, and Late Years of Life.* Pittsburgh: Epiphany Books, 1991.

——— and Susan Muto. *Practicing the Prayer of Presence.* Williston Park, NY: Resurrection Press, 1993.

——— and Susan Muto. *The Power of Appreciation.* New York: Crossroad, 1993.

Vest, Douglas C. *Why Stress Keeps Returning: A Spiritual Response.* Chicago: Loyola University Press, 1991.

von Dürkheim, Karlfried Graf. *Daily Life as Spiritual Exercise: The Way of Transformation*. Trans. Ruth Lewinneck and P. L. Travers. New York: Harper & Row, Publishers, Perennial Library, 1972.

_____. *The Vital Centre of Man*. London: George Allen & Unwin Ltd., 1962.

Williams, Redford. *The Trusting Heart*. New York: Times Books, Div. of Random House, 1989.

Spirit Life Series

*High quality, inexpensive, small books which promote
Christian lifestyles in contemporary settings.*

YOUNG PEOPLE AND . . . YOU KNOW WHAT
Eroding the New Paganism, *by William O'Malley, S.J.*

— For teachers, parents, youth ministers —

Bill O'Malley knows young people — he's been teaching them for over
30 years — and he knows how difficult it is to speak to them about sex.
In this book he provides ways — using reason alone — to outfox teenage
convictions that sex has no human consequences.

"When dealing with sex questions, parents and teachers have to be ex-
traordinarily patient — and loving. . . . We are fighting against an Enemy
who has been entrenched within their minds and value systems since they
were sitting in their Pampers in front of the Electronic Babysitter."

ISBN 1-878718-13-4   40pp.   **$3.50**

———

A powerful sequel to the bestselling Miracle Hour

5-MINUTE MIRACLES
Praying for People with Simplicity and Power, *by Linda Schubert*

"A gift to the Church today. . . . Linda Schubert has undoubtedly birthed
a second miracle! A must read for all who desire to comfort others by
praying with them and for those who have not yet dared to desire."

— Babsie Bleasdell

"Not just a gem, but a treasure-trove of inspiration. . . . Linda Schubert
demonstrates that arm-around-the-shoulder informality plus let's-pray-
about-it compassion can draw five-minute miracles from a God of in-
candescent love."   — John H. Hampsch, C.M.F

LINDA SCHUBERT is the author of *Miracle Hour,* which has sold over
300,000 copies, and is a worldwide speaker on the power of prayer.

ISBN 1-878718-08-8   64pp.   **$3.95**

FAITH MEANS: If Your Pray for Rain, Bring an Umbrella
by Antoinette Bosco

"Antoinette Bosco has taken a mysterious subject — faith — and made it clear and comprehensible. Readers of all ages will finish this little book feeling both challenged and reassured."   — Joan Wester Anderson

ANTOINETTE BOSCO is a syndicated columnist for *Catholic News Service* and the author of five books.

ISBN 1-878718-15-0   48pp.   **$3.50**

NOTHING BUT LOVE: Health and Holiness through Intimacy with God
by Robert E. Lauder

"Sensitively and simply, Father Lauder deals with some of the most profound and mysterious aspects of Christian life: spirituality, prayer and especially the personal presence of God in people's lives. *Nothing but Love* should help many come into closer relationship with the God revealed in Jesus."   — Bernard Cooke

ROBERT LAUDER is a professor of philosophy at St. John's University in Jamaica, NY and the author of eight books.

ISBN 1-878718-16-9   64pp.   **$3.95**

Spirit-Life Audiocassette Collection

Witnessing to Gospel Values *Paul Surlis*	$6.95
Celebrating the Vision of Vatican II *Michael Himes*	$6.95
Hail Virgin Mother *Robert Lauder*	$6.95
Praying on Your Feet *Robert Lauder*	$6.95
Annulment: Healing-Hope-New Life *Thomas Molloy*	$6.95
Life After Divorce *Tom Hartman*	$6.95
Path to Hope *John Dillon*	$6.95
Thank You Lord! *McGuire/DeAngelis*	$8.95

Also published by Resurrection Press

Discovering Your Light *Margaret O'Brien*	$6.95
The Gift of the Dove *Joan M. Jones, PCPA*	$3.95
Healing through the Mass *Robert DeGrandis, SSJ*	$7.95
His Healing Touch *Michael Buckley*	$7.95
Of Life and Love *James P. Lisante*	$5.95
A Celebration of Life *Anthony Padovano*	$7.95
Miracle in the Marketplace *Henry Libersat*	$5.95
Give Them Shelter *Michael Moran*	$6.95
Heart Business *Dolores Torrell*	$6.95
A Path to Hope *John Dillon*	$5.95
The Healing of the Religious Life *Faricy/Blackborow*	$6.95
Transformed by Love *Margaret Magdalen, CSMV*	$5.95
RVC Liturgical Series: The Liturgy of the Hours	$3.95
The Lector's Ministry	$3.95
Our Liturgy	$4.25
The Great Seasons	$3.95
Behold the Man *Judy Marley, SFO*	$3.50
I Shall Be Raised Up	$2.25
From the Weaver's Loom *Donald Hanson*	$7.95
In the Power of the Spirit *Kevin Ranaghan*	$6.95
Lights in the Darkness *Ave Clark, O.P.*	$8.95
Practicing the Prayer of Presence *van Kaam/Muto*	$7.95

Resurrection Press books and cassettes are available in your local religious bookstore. If you want to be on our mailing list for our up-to-date announcements, please write or phone:

Resurrection Press
P.O. Box 248, Williston Park, NY 11596
1-800-89 BOOKS